Blanchette
et les
Sept Petits Cajuns
A Cajun Snow White

Blanchette
et les
Sept Petits Cajuns
A Cajun Snow White

By Sheila Hébert-Collins

Illustrated by Patrick Soper

PELICAN PUBLISHING COMPANY
Gretna 2002

In loving memory of Anthony ("Tony") McLin

Special thanks to Angie McMorris Cornett and her eighth-grade class of 2000 at Frost Elementary in Livingston Parish, Louisiana, for their contributions to this story. Never forget your Cajun roots and continue to write with Cajun pride!

Library of Congress Cataloging-in-Publication Data

Collins, Sheila Hébert.
  Blanchette et les sept petits Cajuns : a Cajun Snow White / written by Sheila Hébert-Collins ; illustrated by Patrick Soper.
      p. cm.
Summary: A Cajun version of Snow White that features a vain voodoo queen, seven little Cajuns living in a cypress tree, and a handsome plantation owner. Includes pronunciations and translations of Cajun words and a recipe for Blanchette's Chicken and Sausage Jambalaya.
  ISBN 1-56554-912-0 (alk. paper)
  [1. Fairy tales. 2. Folklore—Germany.] I. Soper, Patrick, ill. II. Snow White and the seven dwarfs. English. III. Title.
  PZ8.C6953 Ck 2002
  [398.2]—dc21

                    2002005672

French editing by Barbara Hébert Hébert

Printed in Korea

Published by Pelican Publishing Company, Inc.
1000 Burmaster Street, Gretna, Louisiana 70053

BLANCHETTE ET LES SEPT PETITS CAJUNS
A Cajun Snow White

Once upon a time in the Louisiana swamplands, there lived a woman known for her voodoo powers, *Marie Gaudet*. She lived in a cypress hut deep in Honey Island Swamp, where many visited her everyday for some of her *gris gris*.

Marie Gaudet (mah ree go day) Cajun-French name
gris gris (gree gree) magic

Everyday Marie would gather the secret ingredients to make the magic potion that kept her young and beautiful: two possum feet, an egret beak, a frog tongue, and eyes of a moccasin. She'd cook it up, drink a cup, then walk over to the murky waters of Honey Island Swamp and say, "Bayou, bayou, hear my plea. Who's the fairest maiden in the land of the cypress tree?"

The foggy bayou replied:
"*Marie Gaudet* is the fairest I know,
as far as the bayous flow."

But on a day that *Marie Gaudet* will never forget, the murky
waters spoke of her worst fear:
"Black as *nuit* her hair does flow,
lips *très rouge,* and skin like snow.
Blanchette is the fairest I know,
as far as the bayous flow."

nuit (nwee) night
très rouge (tray rooj) very red
Blanchette (blôn shet) "blanche"=French for white

Marie screamed her most terrible scream, called all her creatures of the swamp, and commanded, "Find this *Blanchette* and lead her into my swamp to die." The creatures searched all the plantations around Honey Island Swamp.

Finally, they came upon Armand Plantation, where they found *Blanchette*. With the help of *Marie's gris gris,* the swamp creatures lured her deep into the swamp where she could never find her way home. They all rushed back to *Marie* to tell her of *Blanchette's* fate.

Pauvre bête, Blanchette wandered about the dark swamp, know-ing she would soon be eaten up by swamp creatures, but they all were entranced by her beauty. They only wanted to help her and led her to Cypress Cove, to a large cypress tree covered with moss. Hidden beneath the moss was a little door. *Blanchette* opened the door and found a cute little home. There was a *petite table à manger* made from a cypress stump, with seven little cypress knees for chairs. *La table* was piled high with dirty gumbo bowls and the sink piled high with pots. Her first thought was to clean up, so these *bien petite* people would let her *faire la veillée*.

pauvre bête (poov bet) poor thing
petite table à manger (p'teet tahb ah môn jhay) little dining table
la table (lah tahb) the table
bien petite (bee yehn p'teet) very little
faire la veillée (fair lah vay yay) stay late into the night

After cleaning, *Blanchette* was *bien fatigué,* so she looked around for a bed to *faire dodo.* She found *sept petits* moss beds, each one with a name carved on top. There was one for *Hébert, Mouton, Trahan, Broussard, Hollier, Comeaux,* and *Préjean.*

"Surely these cute little Cajuns will welcome me into their home," she thought. She snuggled into *Préjean's* bed and fell asleep.

bien fatigué (bee yehn fah tee gay) very tired
faire dodo (fair doedoe) go to sleep
sept (set) seven
petit (p'teet) small
Hébert (A bear), *Mouton* (Moo tôn), *Trahan* (Trôn hôn),
    Broussard (Broo sard), *Hollier* (Ohl yay), *Comeaux* (Koe moe),
    Préjean (Pray zhôn) French names

De bon matin, the *sept petits* Cajuns came home from their night of hunting gators. They were surprised to see their home neat and tidy. They washed up, ate some good, fried alligator, then headed for bed. When *Préjean* saw *Blanchette,* he called to his friends. They all watched as she slept.

When *Blanchette* awoke, she told the little Cajuns how she came to be there. *Les petits* Cajuns agreed that *Marie Gaudet* must be at the bottom of this and begged *Blanchette* to stay with them forever so they could protect her. *Blanchette* agreed.

de bon matin (der bôn mah tehn) early in the morning

Everyday *Blanchette* cooked her *petits amis* their favorites, jambalaya or gumbo, and then off they went into the swamp. *Préjean* would remind her, "Do not open *la porte. Marie* will surely be looking for you, *sha.*"

petits amis (p'teet zah me) little friends
la porte (lah port) the door
sha (sha) from the French word, "cher," meaning darling

Avant longtemps, Marie called for her swamp creatures to prepare her potion. She cooked it up then drank a cup. *Marie* then walked to the murky bayou waters of Honey Island Swamp and asked, "Bayou, bayou, hear my plea. Who's the fairest maiden in the land of the cypress tree?"

The bayou waters rose and replied:

"*Marie, Marie,* you are fair, but no, no.

Blanchette is the fairest as far as the bayous flow.

With *sept petits* Cajuns she will be,

living in Cypress Cove in a cypress tree."

avant longtemps (ah vôn lôn tôn) after a while

Again, *Marie* screamed her most terrible scream and called for her swamp creatures. "Prepare my potion," she commanded. " I will fix that *Blanchette* myself." Two possum feet, an egret beak, a frog tongue, and eyes from a moccasin . . . but this time *Marie* added a spell. "Potion, potion, that I need, disguise me for my evil deed." *Marie* drank the potion and was transformed into an old Cajun maw-maw. "Now, I will make a batch of poison *beignets* that no one can resist."

beignets (been yay) square doughnuts with powdered sugar

Marie's swamp creatures led her to the moss-covered cypress tree. She knocked à la porte then called out, "Bonsoir, mes petits amis. I live nearby and brought by a batch of beignets." Blanchette called out that she could not open la porte but she would surely love to have some beignets. So Marie put them on the window ledge and left, feeling sure that the beignets would be eaten.

Bonsoir, mes petits amis. (Bôn swah, may p'teet zah me.)
   Good evening, my little friends.

Sure enough, *Blanchette* quickly bit into those delicious *beignets,* and fell to the floor, lifeless.

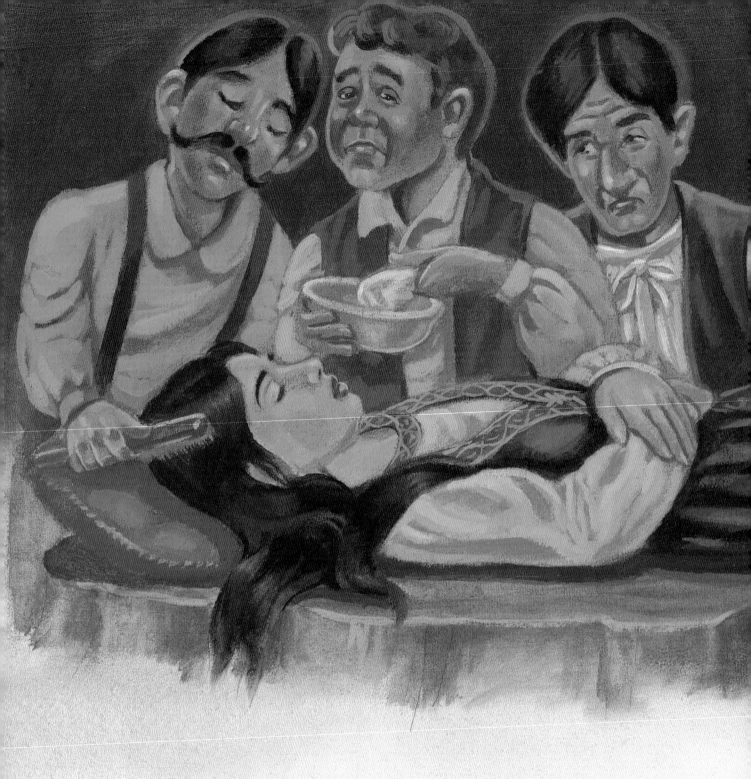

When *les petits* Cajuns came home from their gator hunt, they found *Blanchette,* lifeless. They watched her and cried for three days. Finally, *Préjean* said, "*Mon dieu,* she is still so beautiful. We can certainly not bury her in that cold ground. Let's build a glass box for her and keep it beneath her favorite magnolia tree." And it was done. They visited her everyday.

mon dieu (môn dyu) my goodness

One day, a rich plantation owner, *André Cossé,* came upon the glass box while hunting in the swamp. He sat beside it, entranced by *Blanchette's* beauty.

André Cossé (Ôn dray Coe say) French name

When *les petits* Cajuns discovered him there, they were upset, but they soon realized that he loved her as much as they did. *Monsieur Cossé* begged them to let him take her to *Docteur Briére,* the finest doctor in New Orleans. *Les petits* Cajuns agreed because they didn't want to believe *Blanchette* was really dead.

monsieur (m'syuhr) mister
Docteur Briére (Dawk tur Bree air) French name

Les sept petits Cajuns helped lift the glass box into *Monsieur Cossé's pirogue,* and as they did, a piece of poison *beignet* fell out of *Blanchette's* mouth. *Blanchette* awoke! *Les petits* Cajuns opened the glass box and *Blanchette* stood up slowly, then asked, *"Mais, quoi qu'est arrivé?"*

Les petits Cajuns told *Blanchette* what had happened and that they felt sure it was *Marie's* evil doing.

pirogue (pee rohg) small flat-bottom boat
Mais, quoi qu'est arrivé? (Mehn, qwahs tah ee vay?)
  Well, what's happened?

Suddenly, *Monsieur Cossé* fell to his knees and said, "Marry me and I will protect you forever."

Blanchette fell instantly in love. She kissed *les petits* Cajuns *au revoir* and promised to come back to *faire la veillée.*

au revoir (oh rev wah) good-bye

Marie had heard about *André Cossé's* wedding. She was determined to attend the wedding of the richest plantation owner in all of Cypress Cove to see for herself if his bride was beautiful. So she prepared a special potion to make her even more beautiful: four possum feet, two egret beaks, a nutria tongue, and eyes of moccasin. She cooked it up and drank a cup. She walked to the murky bayou waters and once more asked, "Bayou, bayou, hear my plea. Who is the fairest maiden in the land of the cypress tree?"

The bayou waters rose and replied:
    "Black as *nuit,* her hair does flow,
    lips *très rouge*, and skin like snow.
    Blanchette, the bride of *André Cossé,*
    is the fairest maiden I know, as far as the bayous flow."

Marie screamed her most terrible scream, fainted into the murky swamp waters, and was never seen again.

Blanchette married *André Cossé* that very day. *Les petits* Cajuns walked *Blanchette* down the aisle. *Blanchette* and *André* lived happily ever after, deep in Honey Island Swamp, where her *petite enfants* could see their *sept petits parrains* every day.

C'est tout!

petite enfants (p'teet on fôn) little children
parrains (pah rehn) godfathers
C'est tout! (Say too!) That's all!

BLANCHETTE'S
CHICKEN-AND-SAUSAGE JAMBALAYA

Origin of Jambalaya: Legend tells of how a well-to-do guest arrived late at a New Orleans inn, wanting dinner. The proprietor turned to his chef and said, *"Jean, balayez,"* meaning "blend some good things together." The guest was delighted with the results and asked what it was called. The proprietor said, *"Jean, balayez."* From then on, many ordered *"Jean, balayez."* In time, the words were run together and became known as *Jambalaya.*

2 lbs. deboned chicken pieces
1 lb. smoked pork sausage, sliced
¼ cup oil
1 tsp. Tony's Creole Seasoning
2 tsp. salt
2 celery ribs, chopped
½ cup bell pepper, chopped
2 garlic cloves, chopped
1 can (8 oz.) tomato sauce
2 tbsp. parsley, chopped
2 tbsp. green-onion tops, chopped
4 cups rice, cooked
2 large onions, chopped

Directions: Heat oil in a large, thick pot on medium-high heat. Add chicken, brown, and cook 20 minutes. Add sausage, seasoning, and salt. Cover and cook on low heat for 30 minutes. Remove sausage and chicken. Add onion, celery, bell pepper, and garlic and sauté until tender. Stir in tomato sauce and return chicken and sausage to the pot. Cover and simmer about 10 minutes. Add onion tops and parsley and cook covered for 5 minutes. Fold in cooked rice and simmer about 10 minutes. Serve with French bread and coleslaw. *Bon appétit!*

———————————————,
this is your very own special book!
It was selected for you even before you
were born. It is filled with all the important things
in your life. It is about YOU, your family, your home,
and your world. Do you remember when you were a
tiny little baby? Do you remember when you first crawled
and what your favorite first food was? What made you
laugh when you were little and what made you really, really
mad? What were your favorite games, songs, and books?
the big book of me will remind you. You'll love your
special book when you are two, and you'll love it when
you are all grown-up. Help to fill it in and record
everything from your first five years. We want this book
to show you what a special person
you are and how very
much loved you are.

5" x 7"

the big book of

me

my baby book

Welcome Books

New York • San Francisco

table of contents

In Anticipation

3" x 3"

this is a picture of me in my mommy's belly

My due date was _____

My mommy knew she was pregnant with me _____

She first felt me move inside her belly on _____

I started waking her up at night on _____

My mommy's thoughts while waiting for me: _____

_____

_____

_____

5" x 7"

this is my mommy with me in her belly

Life is always a rich and steady time when you are waiting for something to happen or to hatch.

—*Charlotte's Web*, E. B. White

My Family's History

"If you become a bird and fly away from me," said his mother,
"I will be a tree that you come home to."

—*THE RUNAWAY BUNNY*, MARGARET WISE BROWN

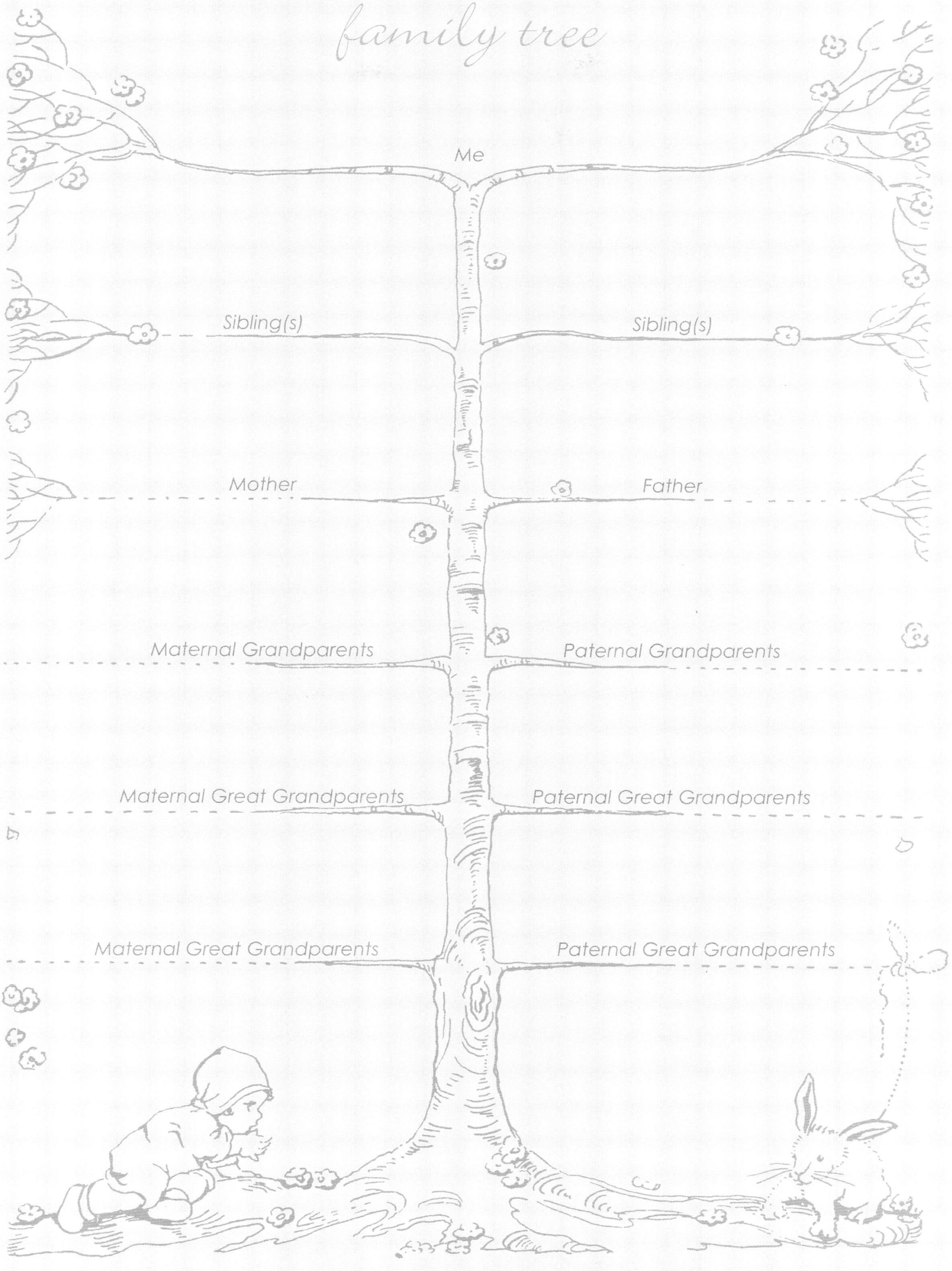

family tree

Me

Sibling(s)

Sibling(s)

Mother

Father

Maternal Grandparents

Paternal Grandparents

Maternal Great Grandparents

Paternal Great Grandparents

Maternal Great Grandparents

Paternal Great Grandparents

My Mommy & Daddy

My mommy's name is
She was born on
She was born in
and raised in
She spends her time

Her favorite things to do are

My daddy's name is _____
He was born on _____
He was born in _____
and raised in _____
He spends his time _____
_____
_____
_____
_____
_____

His favorite things to do are _____
_____
_____
_____
_____
_____
_____
_____

My mommy and daddy met _____
_____
_____
_____
_____
_____
_____

My Grandparents

My dad's mom's name is _____

Her birthdate is _____

She was born in _____

Her interests and hobbies: _____

_____

_____

Her thoughts on being a grandmother: _____

_____

_____

_____

_____

_____

My dad's dad's name is _____

His birthdate is _____

He was born in _____

His interests and hobbies: _____

_____

_____

_____

His thoughts on being a grandfather: _____

_____

_____

_____

_____

How my grandparents met: _____

_____

_____

_____

Nobody can do for little children what grandparents do.
Grandparents sort of sprinkle stardust over the lives of little children.

—ALEX HALEY

My mom's mom's name is _____
Her birthdate is _____
She was born in _____
Her interests and hobbies: _____
_____
_____
_____

Her thoughts on being a grandmother: _____
_____
_____
_____
_____

My mom's dad's name is _____
His birthdate is _____
He was born in _____
His interests and hobbies: _____
_____
_____
_____

His thoughts on being a grandfather: _____
_____
_____
_____
_____

How my grandparents met: _____
_____
_____

My Shower

It was the first party to which Roo
had ever been, and he was very excited.

—*Winnie-the-Pooh*, A. A. Milne

My shower was on _____

It was given by _____
at _____

Guests   Gifts

_____   _____

_____   _____

_____   _____

_____   _____

_____   _____

_____   _____

_____   _____

_____   _____

_____   _____

_____   _____

_____   _____

_____   _____

_____   _____

_____   _____

_____   _____

_____   _____

Thoughts and wishes of family and friends

I Arrive!

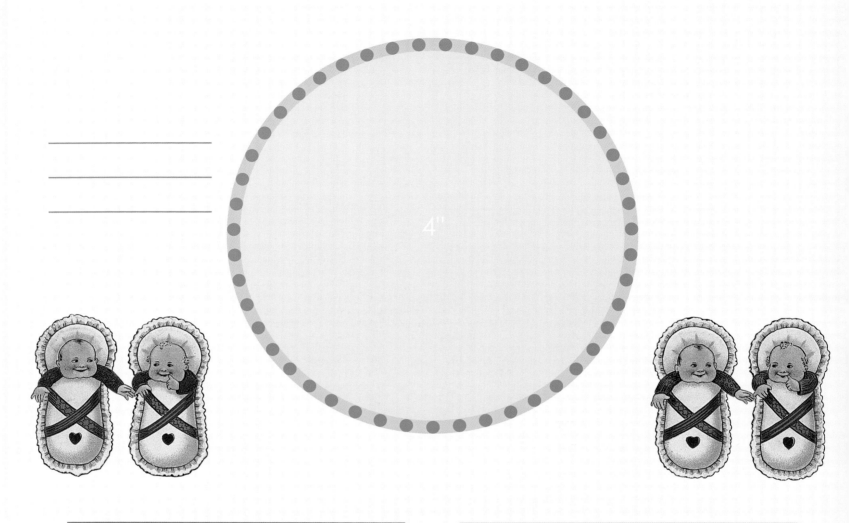

4"

3¼" x 3¼"

3¼" x 3¼"

A person's a person, no matter how small.

—Dr. Seuss

My name is _____

_____ .

I was born on _____

at _____ o'clock

in _____

_____ .

I weighed _____ .

I measured _____ in length

and _____ in head circumference.

I had _____ hair and _____ eyes

and a _____ wail.

Memories

_____
_____
_____
_____
_____
_____
_____
_____
_____
_____
_____
_____
_____
_____
_____
_____
_____
_____
_____
_____
_____
_____
_____

My Baby Announcement

The first cry of a newborn baby in Chicago or Zamboango,
in Amsterdam or Rangoon, has the same pitch and key, each saying,
"I am! I have come through! I belong! I am a member of the Family!

—CARL SANDBURG

paste baby anouncement here

Predictions

And will you succeed?
Yes! You will, indeed!
(98 and 3/4 percent guaranteed.)

—*Oh, the Places You'll Go!*, Dr. Seuss

My Astrological sign is _____
Some characteristics of my sign are

_____
_____
_____
_____
_____
_____
_____
_____
_____
_____
_____

My birthstone is _____

Predictions by family and friends:

_____
_____
_____
_____
_____
_____
_____
_____

Little Bits of Me

I started teething on _____
I got my first tooth on _____
I got my second tooth on _____

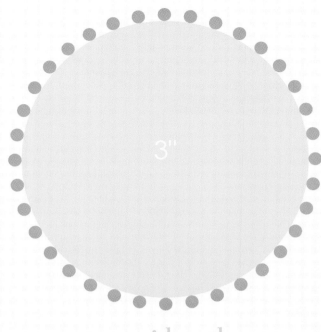

me with teeth

a lock of my hair

Everybody says my hair is just like _____
_____
_____
_____

I had my first haircut on _____

20

This little piggy went to market,
This little piggy stayed home,
This little piggy had roast beef,
This little piggy had none,
And this little piggy cried,
Wee, wee, wee, all the way home.

Handprints and Footprints

left hand   right hand

left foot   right foot

21

My World

When I was born important world events were _____
_____
_____
_____

The president was _____
The music Mommy and Daddy were listening to was _____
_____

Their favorite movies and television shows were _____
_____
_____

Exciting sports events were _____
_____
_____

The price of things:
postage stamp _____   gasoline _____
milk _____   college _____
newspaper _____   other _____

Other signs of the times were _____
_____
_____
_____
_____

The five little puppies dug a
hole under the fence . . .
and went for a walk in the
wide, wide world.
—*THE POKY LITTLE PUPPY*

Home

The third little pig worked from morning til night and built himself a beautiful house of bricks.

—THE THREE LITTLE PIGS

My address is _____

_____

I live with _____

_____

The favorite things in my room are _____

_____

_____

_____

Things I love to do at home are _____

_____

_____

_____

_____

_____

_____

My favorite neighborhood places and outings are _____

_____

_____

_____

_____

_____

_____

_____

Record of Growth

Mary, Mary, quite contrary,
How does your garden grow?
With silver bells and cockleshells,
And pretty maids all in a row.

—MOTHER GOOSE

age	weight	height
1 week		
2 weeks		
1 month		
2 months		
3 months		
5 months		
7 months		
9 months		
1 year		
18 months		
2 years		
3 years		
4 years		
5 years		

3½" x 5"

little me

3½" x 5"

medium me

3½" x 5"

big me!

My First Time

Smiling _____
Holding head up _____
Rolling over _____
Laughing _____
Sitting up _____
Eating solid food _____
Crawling _____
Standing up _____

Playing peekaboo _____
Waving bye-bye _____
Stepping _____
Talking _____
Walking _____
Climbing up stairs _____
Running _____
Humming and singing

Other great achievements _____

_____
_____
_____
_____
_____
_____
_____
_____
_____

When the first baby laughed for the first time,
the laugh broke into a thousand pieces
and they all went skipping about,
and that was the beginning of fairies

—J. M. BARRIE

I smiled for the first time at _____

_____

I laughed out loud for the first time when _____

_____

My first solid food was _____

_____

I took my first steps toward _____

_____

My first words and sentences were _____

_____

_____

3½" x 3½"

3"

_____   _____

_____   _____

_____   _____

Sweet Dreams

3½" × 5"

a little angel

I finally slept through the night on _____

My favorite things for bedtime are _____

_____

_____

_____

_____

_____

_____

Some of my mommy and daddy's thoughts and dreams when I was little:

_____
_____
_____
_____
_____
_____
_____
_____
_____
_____
_____
_____
_____
_____
_____
_____
_____
_____
_____
_____
_____
_____

Wynken and Blynken are two little eyes,

And Nod is a little head,

And the wooden shoe that sailed the skies

Is a wee one's trundle-bed.

So shut your eyes while mother sings

Of wonderful sights that be,

And you shall see the beautiful things

As you rock in the misty sea . . .

—Eugene Field

Favorite Things

The world is so full of a number of things,
I'm sure we should all be as happy as kings.

—ROBERT LOUIS STEVENSON

My favorite toys: _____
_____
_____

My favorite games: _____
_____
_____

My favorite books: _____
_____
_____

My favorite rhymes: _____
_____
_____

My favorite television shows and videos: _____
_____
_____

Other favorite things: _____
_____
_____
_____
_____
_____

3½" x 5"

_____

_____

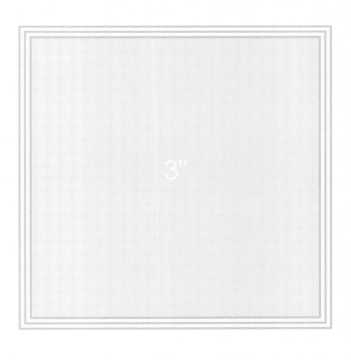

3"

3"

_____

_____

_____

_____

_____

_____

That's Funny!

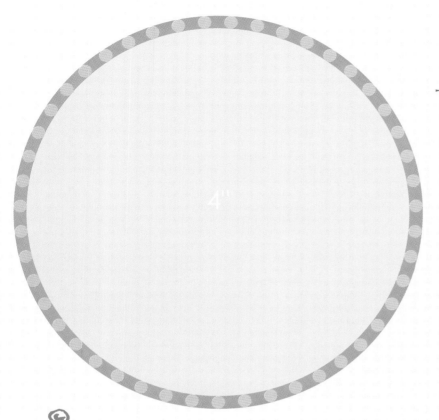

4"

Hey, diddle diddle!
The cat and the fiddle,
The cow jumped over the moon,
The little dog laughed
To see such sport,
And the dish ran away
with the spoon.

—MOTHER GOOSE

_____

_____

_____

What makes me laugh:

_____
_____
_____
_____
_____
_____
_____
_____
_____
_____
_____
_____

I'm Mad!

"But I don't want to go among mad people," said Alice.
"Oh, you can't help that," said the cat. "We're all mad here."

—*ALICE'S ADVENTURES IN WONDERLAND, LEWIS CARROLL*

Things that make me sad: _____
_____

Things that make me mad: _____
_____

When I am mad I _____
_____

I always feel better when _____
_____

3½" x 5"

_____

Bathtime

Rub-a-dub-dub, three men in a tub,
The butcher, the baker, the candlestick maker.

—MOTHER GOOSE

I took my first bath on _____
My favorite water toys are _____

_____

At bathtime, I love _____

_____

_____

_____

_____

_____

_____

_____

3¹/₂" x 5"

I Love Food!

3½" x 5"

_____

_____

_____

My favorite things to eat are _____

_____

_____

_____

I really don't like _____

_____

_____

_____

Say! I like green eggs and ham! I do! I like them, Sam-I-am!

—GREEN EGGS AND HAM, DR. SEUSS

Musical Me

My favorite songs are _____

_____

_____

_____

_____

_____

I like making music with _____

_____

_____

_____

_____

_____

The first time I danced to music _____

_____

_____

_____

_____

Oh, the wonderful sounds
Mr. Brown can do.
Why don't you try
to do them too?

—MR. BROWN CAN MOO! CAN YOU?,
DR. SEUSS

My Artworks

And he set off on his walk,
taking his big purple crayon with him.

—*Harold and the Purple Crayon*,
Crockett Johnson

My first attempts at art: _____

_____

My mom's praises: _____

_____

_____

paste masterpiece here

Record of Cute Sayings

Date   Sayings

& Sensible Remarks

Date   Sayings

"The time has come," the Walrus said,
"to talk of many things: Of shoes—
and ships—and sealing wax—
Of cabbages—and kings . . ."

—THROUGH THE LOOKING GLASS,
LEWIS CARROLL

Mommy and Me

The favorite things I like to do with Mommy are _____

_____

_____

_____

_____

_____

_____

_____

_____

_____

4" x 6"

_____

*And Max the King of all wild things was lonely
and wanted to be where someone loved him best of all.*
—*WHERE THE WILD THINGS ARE*, MAURICE SENDAK

A letter from my mommy to me

_____

_____

_____

_____

_____

_____

_____

_____

_____

_____

_____

_____

_____

_____

_____

_____

_____

_____

_____

_____

_____

_____

_____

_____

_____

_____

_____

_____

_____

_____

_____

_____

Daddy and Me

4" x 6"

H OP POP

We like to hop
We like to hop
on top of Pop.

—HOP ON POP, DR. SEUSS

The favorite things I like to do with Daddy are _____

_____

_____

_____

_____

_____

A letter from my daddy to me

My Family and Me

A family is
everybody all together.

—*A Baby Sister for Frances*,
Russel Hoban

The special members of my family are _____
_____
_____
_____
_____
_____

The favorite things I do with them are _____
_____
_____
_____
_____
_____
_____
_____
_____
_____
_____
_____
_____
_____

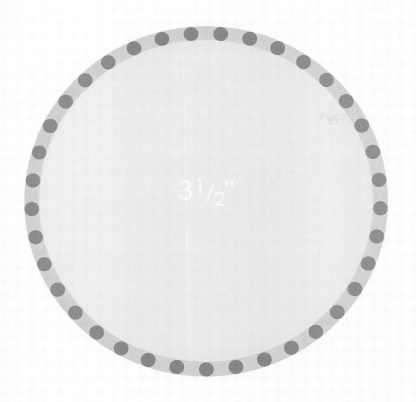

3¹/₂"

3¹/₂" x 3¹/₂"

4" x 6"

Best Friends

name _____

age _____

things we do _____

_____

_____

_____

_____

_____

_____

_____

_____

_____

_____

_____

name _____

age _____

things we do _____

_____

_____

_____

_____

_____

_____

_____

_____

_____

_____

_____

"You have been my friend. That in itself is a tremendous thing."

—CHARLOTTE'S WEB, E. B. WHITE

name _____

age _____

things we do _____

_____

_____

_____

_____

_____

_____

_____

_____

_____

_____

name _____

age _____

things we do _____

_____

_____

_____

_____

_____

_____

_____

_____

_____

_____

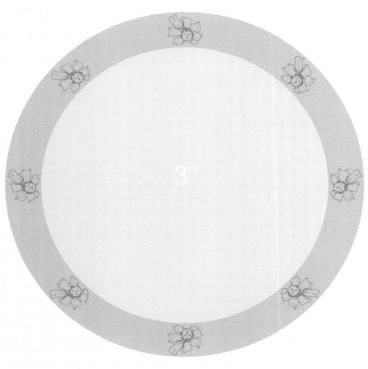

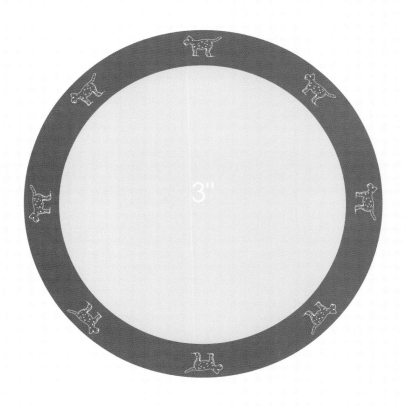

I Am What I Am!

When I was a year old, I had these character traits: _____
_____
_____
_____
_____
_____

My daddy says I remind him of _____
_____
_____
_____
_____
_____
_____
_____
_____

My mommy says I remind her of _____
_____
_____
_____
_____
_____
_____
_____
_____
_____

He was a good little monkey and always very curious.

—CURIOUS GEORGE, H. A. REY

Things I am very good at are _____

_____

_____

_____

_____

_____

_____

_____

_____

_____

_____

_____

_____

_____

_____

_____

_____

_____

Things I need to work on are _____

_____

_____

_____

_____

_____

_____

_____

_____

_____

_____

_____

_____

_____

_____

It's Spring

4" x 6"

The special things I do in the spring: _____
_____
_____
_____
_____
_____
_____
_____
_____
_____
_____
_____
_____
_____

Spring is showery, flowery, bowery . . .

Summertime Fun

The fun things I do during the summer: _____

_____

_____

_____

_____

_____

_____

_____

_____

_____

_____

_____

4" x 6"

Summer: hoppy, croppy, poppy . . .

It's Fall

The special things I do in the fall: _____
_____
_____
_____
_____
_____
_____
_____
_____
_____
_____
_____
_____
_____

4" x 6"

Autumn: wheezy, sneezy, freezy . . .

Wintertime Fun

4" x 6"

The special things I do in the winter: _____
_____
_____
_____
_____
_____
_____
_____
_____
_____
_____
_____
_____
_____
_____

Winter: slippy, drippy, nippy.
—MOTHER GOOSE

Outings

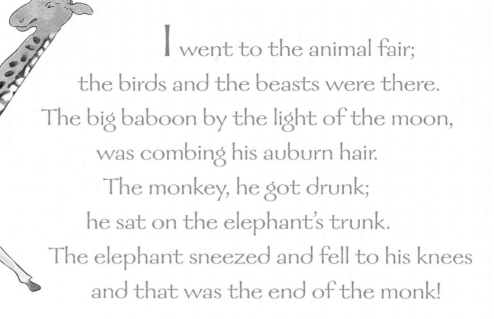

I went to the animal fair;
the birds and the beasts were there.
The big baboon by the light of the moon,
was combing his auburn hair.
The monkey, he got drunk;
he sat on the elephant's trunk.
The elephant sneezed and fell to his knees
and that was the end of the monk!

4" x 6"

_____

_____

_____

_____

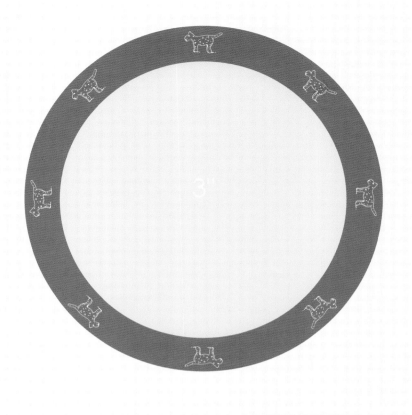

3"

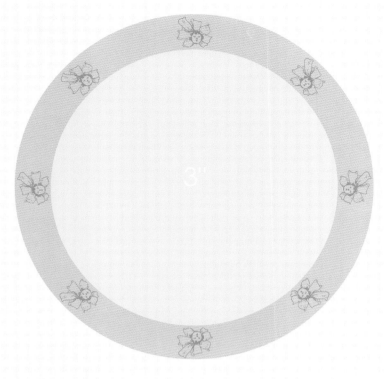

3"

3¹/₂" X 3¹/₂"

3¹/₂" X 3¹/₂"

Travels

4" x 6"

"Second to the right,
and straight on til morning."

—*Peter Pan*, J. M. Barrie

4" x 6"

_____

_____

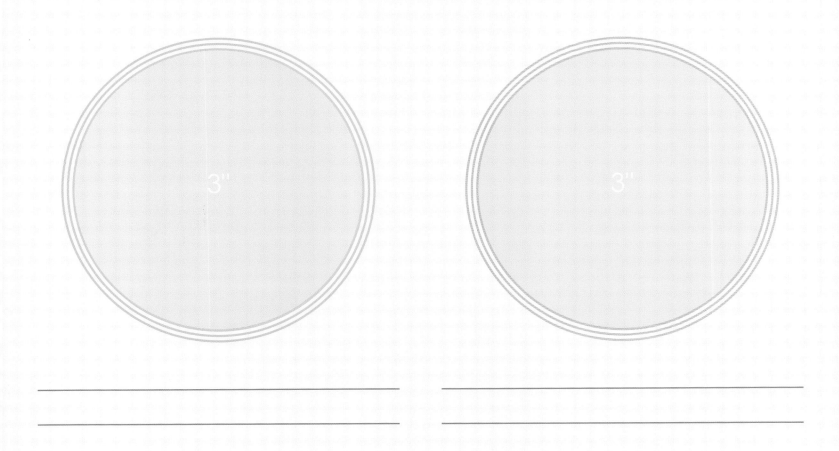

3"

3"

_____

_____

_____

Travels

3" x 3"

3" x 3"

3"

3"

4" x 6"

_____

_____

_____

"I have a new space helmet.
I am going to the moon,"
said Little Bear to Mother Bear.

—LITTLE BEAR,
ELSE HOLMELUND MINARIK

Holidays & Special Events

4" × 6"

special day: _____

memories: _____

_____

_____

_____

The guests have gone home, happy, though tired . . .
They will long remember this great celebration.

—THE STORY OF BABAR, JEAN DE BRUNHOFF

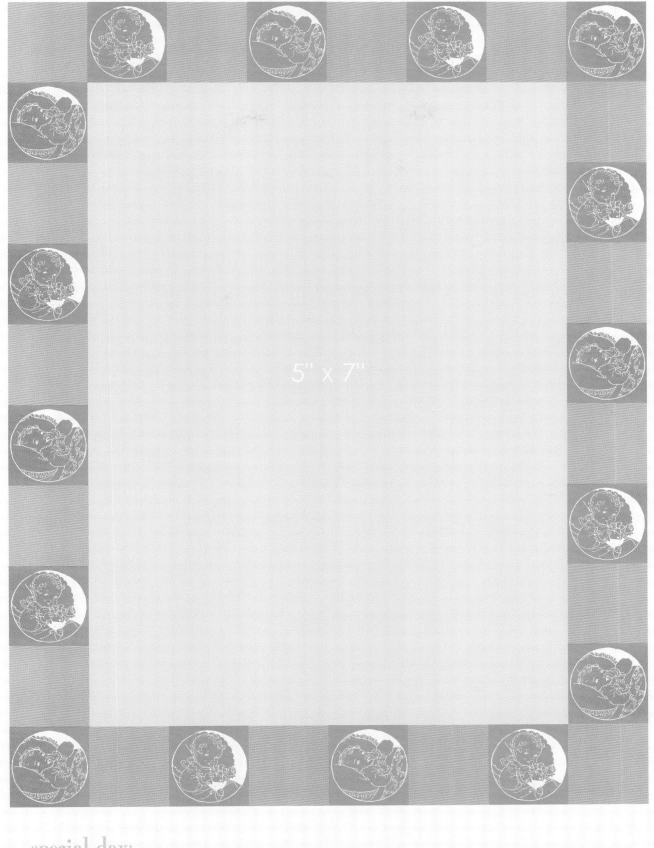

5" x 7"

special day: _____

memories: _____

_____

_____

_____

_____

Holidays & Special Events

special day: _____

_____

memories: _____

_____

_____

_____

3"

3¹/₄" x 3¹/₄"

3¹/₄" x 3¹/₄"

special day: _____

memories: _____

_____

_____

3½" x 5"

special day: _____

memories: _____

_____

_____

3"

3"

special day: _____

memories: _____

_____

_____

Holidays & Special Events

special day: _____

_____

memories: _____

_____

_____

_____

3"

4" x 6"

special day: _____

memories: _____

_____

_____

3¹/₂" x 5"

special day: _____

memories: _____

_____

_____

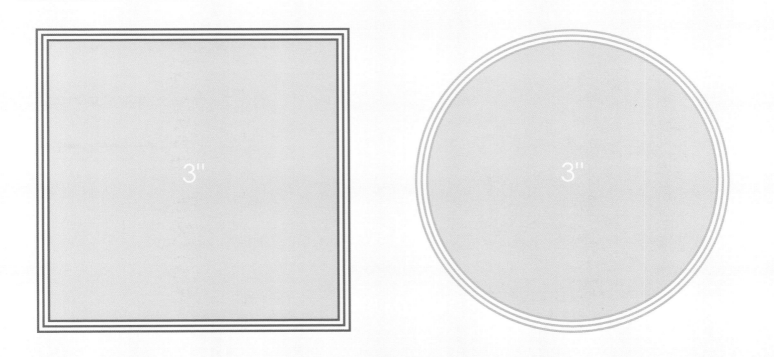

3"

3"

special day: _____

memories: _____

_____

_____

Me, Month by Month

Date   Notes

I can't go back to yesterday because I was a different person then.

—*THROUGH THE LOOKING GLASS*, LEWIS CARROLL

Date   Notes

Me, Month by Month

Date   Notes

_____

_____

_____

_____

_____

_____

_____

_____

_____

_____

_____

_____

_____

_____

_____

_____

_____

_____

Date　　　　　Notes

My First Birthday

I celebrated my first birthday on _____
_____

The party was at _____
_____
_____

My guests included _____
_____
_____
_____
_____

My favorite presents were _____
_____
_____
_____

I am one years old now! The amazing things I can do are ___
_____
_____
_____
_____
_____
_____
_____
_____
_____
_____
_____
_____
_____

3¹/₂" x 3¹/₂"

3¹/₂" x 3¹/₂"

"It's my birthday.
The happiest day of the year."

—EEYORE, *WINNIE-THE-POOH*, A. A. MILNE

4" x 6"

I'm Two!

We celebrated my second birthday _____

_____

_____

_____

I am two years old now! The amazing things I can do are _____

_____

_____

_____

_____

_____

_____

4" x 6"

I'm Three!

4" x 6"

We celebrated my third birthday _____

_____

_____

_____

_____

I am three years old now! The amazing things I can do are

_____

_____

_____

_____

_____

_____

_____

I'm Four!

We celebrated my fourth birthday _____
_____
_____
_____
_____

I am four years old now! The amazing things I can do are
_____
_____
_____
_____
_____
_____
_____

4" X 6"

I'm Five!

All children, except one, grow up.

—Peter Pan, J. M. Barrie

4" x 6"

We celebrated my fifth birthday _____

_____

_____

_____

_____

I am five years old now! The amazing things I can do are

_____

_____

_____

_____

_____

_____

_____

So Much to Remember

4" x 6"

_____

_____

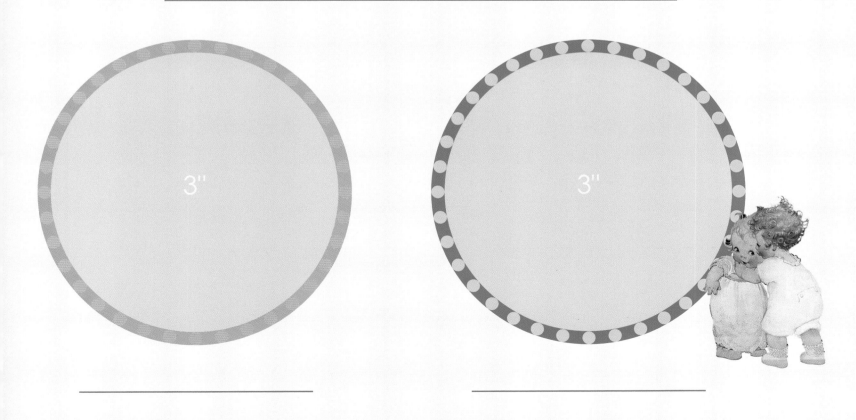

3"

3"

_____   _____

_____   _____

So Much to Remember

4" x 6"

3"

Published in 2005 by Welcome Books®
An imprint of Welcome Enterprises, Inc.
6 West 18th Street
New York, NY 10011
(212) 989-3200; Fax (212) 989-3205
www.welcomebooks.com

Text by Alice Wong
Designed by Naomi Irie

Illustrations Credits

Back cover: Hilda Austin; page 4: Edna Cooke; page 20: P. Ebner; pages 23, 26, 41, 52, 56, 69: Rosie O'neil; page 25: C. M. Burd; page 34: Pete Fraser; page 35: E. Curtis; page 46: Charlotte Becker; page 54: Margaret Evans Price; page 60: H. Q. C. Marsh; page 67: G. G. Drayton; page 73: C. Twelvetrees; page 77: Torre Bevans.

Library of Congress Cataloging-in-Publication Data on file.

ISBN-10: 1-932183-83-3
ISBN-13: 978-1-932183-83-2

Printed in China

First Edition

1 3 5 7 9 10 8 6 4 2

I kiss you and kiss you,
With arms 'round my own,
Ah, how shall I miss you,
When, dear, you have grown.

—WILLIAM BUTLER YEATS